FORM / FORCE

FORM / FORCE
ISBN 978-0-9860050-3-9

(cc) CREATIVE COMMONS SA LICENSE 2.5

KARL LARSSON
BLACK SQUARE EDITIONS

DESIGN / PASCAL PROŠEK • KARL LARSSON • JONAS FRIDÉN

PRINT / USA / 2015

FIRST EDITION

BSE BOOKS ARE DISTRIBUTED BY SPD
Small Press Distribution
1341 Seventh Street
Berkeley, California 94710

1-800-869-7553
orders@spdbooks.org
www.spdbooks.org

TO CONTACT THE PRESS, PLEASE WRITE
Black Square Editions
1200 Broadway, Suite 3C
New York, New York 10001

An Independent Subsidiary of Off The Park Press

The poem excerpts quoted in "Awake from Sleep" are taken from *Cancer in My Left Ball* by John Giorno (Something Else Press, 1973)

FORM / FORCE
KARL LARSSON

Translated by Jennifer Hayashida

WHAT ANDREAS BAADER SAID

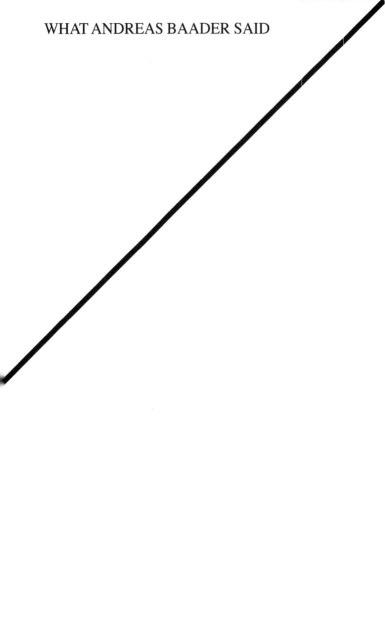

"SO GIVE ME THE MACHINE
GIVE ME THE MONEY
ABOVE ALL GIVE ME POLITICAL POWER"

in february 2003
a mexican man tries
to smuggle himself across the border to the u.s.
disguised as a car seat

the commentary to the monument
nobody's car trip
the state is awakened by violence every morning
somebody's assassination

images from the rest of the world
the map is everywhere
what has happened is archived

search tool, then "mexican + car seat"
the distance between here and there
is long since gone
the body contorts
sewn into the synthetic leather material
quiet, a single night
of inhuman form

sculptures are crushed
and move across the world
(iraq museum in bagdad looted)
unintentionally realized in kabul
adolf loos' dream
of heavy motorized vehicles
plowing down the streets
so the houses quake and façade
ornamentation crashes to the ground

(a dream for vienna, but still)
petrifying glance
the world's myths calibrate
destruction and loss
a mexican man
fills up a second skin
and has an armrest for an arm
in sweeping gestures one can
grasp the terror in the world
in glimpses, now and then, one can see
how everything collapses
(to never be rebuilt)
and is built again at that very moment

the glance that petrifies is embarrassing
on the border between countries the body is discovered
by a newly awakened, laughing border patrol

a format that activates

holger mein's prose
in bo cavefors' translation

what is to be highlighted of raf:s project is
the conviction and the raw communication
the final prison texts convey
there are no capitals other than
THE PIGS and THE STRUGGLE GOES ON
an important word is written
w a r
m a t e r i a l
t o g e t h e r

for the others
a typographic consistency is applied

coherent with the political conviction
the writing conveys
and in places is the same thing
as the meaning of the texts
that is to say structure and stylistics
authority, energy, consumption

one can understand the image of the violence
but not exactly which (image of violence)

to combine materials
within delineated bodies
and to combine bodies
as a fuel for activity

to extend one's hand
a violent text

the book object is placed
against the elusive authority
of the human body
in a book beyond the book
an unbound dream which
takes shape (at) (in)

terracotta, realistic audience
the sculpture collections
"the mass is principally f o r revolt"
how is one to find the ways out necessary
for individual engagement
in this border intermezzo

to begin with the body
with the book and the image
to begin with what takes form

12

(to take form) and gives form (to give form)
the glance that petrifies
belongs to individual groupings
the mass is so large
it takes form and is formless, liquid
firm until it starts to be processed
to write on it, in it
this mass that is now written upon
what takes form and takes life
happens in another place
and is not discovered until at the border
between taxonomies
determined by ownership

the room with the sculptures, past the entrance
in the room where guards discretely explain
that one may no longer stop and talk

(but must constantly circulate)
loneliness arises in the viewer
one among others, unknown epoch
who will find the body
lift it out of the dust
restore …
read it again and again it is new
it is old read it again and again

the alliance between critics is secured
common sense rules
meaning becomes clear

in the first room,
which must be society,
there is consensus about
the necessity of the other room

"sculpture is what you bump into
when you back up
to see a painting"

during friendship, an alliance
anything can happen
one notices one's dual responsibility
to the first room (oneself)
and the other

a violent alliance for freedom
both germany and america
are countries beyond the border

what arises in a specific room
can potentially happen everywhere
one usually distinguishes between base and statue

pedestal and bust
the transition between actual place
and representative sign

a book has a front, a back,
spine, cover, pages
or as the sales people write:
rear board
spine
dust-jacket (dj)
first free end paper (ffep)
(purple) cloth binding
etc.

"spine clearly worn from reading.
dj sunned, with tiny tears"

in a familial belonging anything can happen
one waits for a dual body
for the book, the section
relationship
the terrorist group knows love
for the audience
at the opening it was almost impossible to get through
everyone was there

t h e   c o n d i t i o n s   i n   j a i l
even in what a swedish author
at one point in a blm-interview (1984) calls
"the ideal space"
so, the theater stage
separated from reality
so, the theater stage
with its own theorizing, separate from

the street, life outside
"one sees as through a mirror"
so, the stage
so, t h e   c o n d i t i o n s   i n   j a i l
are different from those that apply
on the street, in life outside
one sees as through a mirror
not with a direct glance but via reference
it is simple to mean one thing and do another
to both do and mean but still not mean
to do something that one then must
see as through a mirror
if one can, if one knows
how one should see in that way
nothing is simple
andreas: "not even speaking to the group
remains simple"

the attack comes from outside
and occupies symbolically
in order for the earlier borders to remain
how important is it now to feel
sorrow over a lost critical discourse

distribution
casting in double materials
even in poetry prose is revealed
to avoid direct pain
(as individual)
or to begin the reading
against one's own body
and finally pass the critical point
when the meeting is with
legions, anyone
processed and practiced

resistance and productive activity
hard and soft materials
it is possible to treat another person
as a sculptural element
one cannot remove the cover
the back (spine), ffep
and title, the author's name and
still maintain the "book-like"
in the book

to establish a position that makes
further reading possible
in the work and its interpretation
there is no longer a radiant
interior light, an aristotelian *eidos*,
which makes it possible to work semantically
and possible to explain

the semantic in the work
different inertia in the ways to witness
the marble body
the book excerpt
the book product
and not least that which
the american book industry terms beach book

a book large and heavy enough to
"prevent a beach towel
from being gone with the wind"

to lay something on something else
so that it finally
is possible to weigh the interaction,
the deep narratives
physically

raf:s cast of characters, the weight
of the texts
that are almost
impossible to get a hold of
bo cavefors' edition has been provided
with portraits of the perpetrators
beautiful young faces
radiate conviction and awareness
of the graininess, the photographic body
within the melancholia of representation

there was someone in the group
who was not "der einzelkämpfer"
someone was clingy
and wrote: *andreas, andreas*
as if andreas had remained
the same also afterwards

the practical application
of t h e s t r u g g l e

to read (is it)
to stare
at what does not exist
strength, solidarity
in the readership

would activism and literature
be possible to unite
without the impossible loneliness

the book: *raf: texts*
august 1977
(c) raf/brd, c/o internationales komitee
zur verteidigung politischer

gefangener in westeuropa
– sektion brd.
isbn 91-504-0651-5
all information
a judicial process
put the publishing house
bo cavefors
into bankruptcy

but before that the book was printed in german
with a new cover
and an assumed, new identity
from three publishers
one could read
love with complications by per a. rosenberg
on any street in berlin
and stuttgart, stammheim prison

still held the prisoners
who would die in october that same year

an external form anticipates
a form of being
per a. rosenberg's body is disowned
not by family and friends
a smuggled-in pistol, the rope
what is by some called suicide
was perhaps not suicide
but serial killings of young german prosaists

there is a fictionalization zone
where the authorial identity
no longer means anything

how is one to represent action

afa,
ira,
raf,
etc.
must still be too literal

if this is a man
what then does a reader mean
the book does not lose form in the same way
as the human archive
it is a part of

how is the radical prose reached
the format that activates
(the author: it is no longer
i who speak
it is someone else

who speaks through me
– *finally)*

finally they are visible
the sculptural qualities in

(break through)
(break through)

when a ruptured body cannot
be retrieved in the book
relevant passages of a book
are no longer in the book

an open darkness
between
identities

the time as reader is gone
in the baader-meinhof gruppe
do not confuse the most important
to shoot people, no
to break up and no longer act
no, to become die gruppe
death to materialism, to die gruppe
to disappear and come
back as icons
to come back as signs
rosetta stones,
surviving materia

the alliance
between state and individual
call it what you will
between state and individual

nothing exists outside the book
that does not in itself
constitute its limits
perhaps it is redundant
to speak of embodiment
when the relationship between
genetic creature and sculpture
is maintained by forces
rhetorically stronger than those
that transformed ohnesorg
to a bundle of meat

with immobility is also meant
loss of the
reflective potential
that is simply called
critical thinking

imagined reunion
the face itself
the myth's reflection
before the joining
with plaster casts from
the periphery of the collections

from the red room
high treason
which one can call
the interior human body
a thick, dark ink is extracted
when the state fiction finally
starts to erode in its genre

fraction group fracture
from preparedness, this
n o w

DOCUMENTATION /
PERFORMANCE (1980) /
RE-LISTENING (2007)

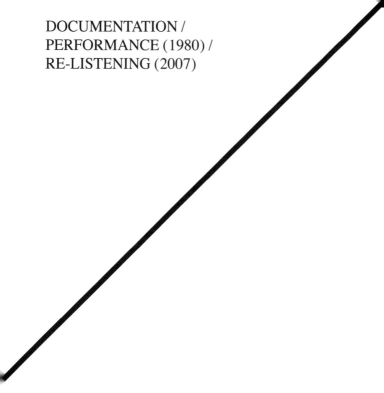

1, 2, 3
it is a good sound,
good sound
nine out of ten

use the body as a vessel
or use the poem as a vessel
or use the story about someone
or something as a vessel

a hollow container (to be filled with ...)

in assumed form
across the invisible borders
that separate realities
economies, languages

there is an image, published
in the danish newspaper jyllands-posten,
depicting a truck
photographed with an x-ray camera
and its cargo, bananas
one can see the bunches,
even individual fruit
and among all these crates
also people
crouching, extended and *x-ray grey*

ian curtis, singer
in the post-punk band joy division
now this sudden image

reading is sometimes only a state,
the neck at a particular angle

what moves has a contents
the eyes' darkness streams in
and blocks the chronic gateways
through which cells of a new kind shall pass
that is to say rebirth the body (in intervals)
during the morning's deep sleep
the entire organism reads
growth hormones, edifying chemistry,
space-time images

the dream's capsule
counteracts
the demands for representation

death large repetition
pursues the form
ian curtis

in the terrible image that has been created
a text is produced, without other meaning
than *hearts fail, young hearts fail*

the body's audiological self-control
an almost worthless diamond
extracted from several tons of black sludge
reaches the engraved surface
it is especially difficult to listen to:

it all falls apart at first touch
its poetry or reality

at the center of the poem the stereo system will stand
and hiss with its voltage
a turntable, the blood

will listen to the music

0. unknown voice intro
right, we all start when the drum machine starts, lads

1. the very first beats
technology fails
while the voice dives
deep below the nazi-
aggressive bass

a concert is also
an abstract sound wave
with breaks for responses,
fictionalization,
through the sea of the audience

so many hands
room full of people,
room for just one
other words

2. the conditions for
the performance
were for ian curtis
to get it together,
not think so much,
not jerk around
but step into the epilepsy
naturally
like an outer layer
totally reflective body
limited,
counted in

musicality is audible
it comes from within,
from the music
suddenly it is difficult to discern
media from one another
the recording's soft,
painterly quality
image and action
licht und blindheit
a flash that appears
every sixtieth second
never ceases to darken
in the photographs remain
a light from the past

3. when the drum machine starts
the body comes back

it makes its way back
the fatigue varies and becomes noise
everything comes back, grows
everything grows and becomes noise
and becomes a good sound
a real noise

the fatigue returns and grows
and becomes a good fatigue
and varies and becomes noise
a real noise
that comes back and makes its way
into the body and returns
as a really good sound

a really good sound now
that grows with the body

the fatigue varies with the noise
that grows with the sound
and it is really good
really good

the body is really tired now
really good
the fatigue makes its way back
the body comes back
and grows and becomes really tired
and becomes a good, varied sound
a real noise and a good sound
like good noise and good sound again

the body tires and comes back
and tires and comes back
the noise returns

to the body again
tires and is really tired
and comes back
grows and becomes a noise

everything grows and becomes real
the body's sound again
a real noise becomes real
the noise comes back
like the fatigue comes back
comes the noise
and the fatigue
the noise and real noise again

4. the book is not over
it is becoming
there is a lot of space left

for what will never
happen

perhaps there is no way
to avoid the fiction

joy division plays
the moonlight club
4/4 1980
what is there to explain
in the nine songs performed
everything is avoided

in the documentary experience,
the reading
one can perceive
a meek presence

but isn't it really
something else
reflected back
from the pages' white anemia
vague absence
by the light of what
could have been shared

the longest song
never ends
the entire machinery's
incomprehensible coordination
does not collapse
until the audience as a whole has interpreted
the untranslatable character set
stored in
the back rooms, dressing rooms

where also the negative image,
the rayogram
of the original group is archived

in the longest song,
the sections that transition
to monotonous non-partiture
virtuosity expires
work remains
as heavy, dark force

the impossibility of
both writing and describing
iconography from within
when nothing
can mean something
for the first time

repeated times during the evening
the group attempts
to articulate four four
nineteen hundred and eighty

the material is so charged
that it revolts within the document
and appears as raw, white sound
liberated from all symbolic weight

the force that activates the machine
could belong to
any society

the microphone is a black sea
concentrated to a drop of the present
cold, clean vocal ocean

in the middle of the poem
should stand recording equipment
turned on or off
documentation is underway
of the quietest variety
no one should be able to differentiate
between what happens
and what does not happen
here

5. the singer dies
by his own hand, in his home
and replaces one economy
with another

the voice fails the poem
at this point

an oral disappointment
the outsiderness of documentation
in the metaphor

in the example joy division
there is in part this song,
number five – *shadowplay*,
in part the music heard
afterward, behind the transparent layer
of abstract expressionism
which in its theoretical construction assumes
that there somewhere in all cultural material
can be defined
absolute punctuation marks, endings

what is heard in silence
is not the original sound

but its contemporary source
one listens to the documentation
of the documentation
and becomes part of the static,
the generational loss

the neck is injured
in the action
the resonance of the hanging
the base, the event itself
takes the form of an arm
its uncontrolled jerking
accounts for
the entire body's death
in the decision's
recurring
moments

he hung himself in the attic
since he could not bear
to live with his cancer

he hung himself in the laundry room
because he lived a double life
and was sleeping with two different women at the
same time

he hung himself in the work room
with iggy pop's *the idiot*
spinning on the turntable

he stood on a block of ice with
piano wire around his neck
when the ice melted he was slowly strangled
because he, because he

ian curtis
runs between the categories
like *ichor*

an attempt to understand the paralysis
the post-production of civil society
why the iconification is so important

how the darkness in the music, by the light of the myth
once again can be so alive
and sadistically liberatory

6. "in the future no one will be famous"
– anonymous

more than halfway into the recording
one can no longer discern

the specific beat

memory of the particular
has merged with
the experience of similarity

the body could belong
to anyone

the temptation to step down into
identitylessness
and feel tongue, pharynx, throat
cavities for resonance
the need to have one's name
converted into sound
to be able to leave
the solitude of a rare form

and become part of the collections

the classification of the private
is made at the expense of the group
the communal ceases
social support is no longer an
obvious resource
but a consequence of individual
failure

the book can be printed
in an infinite number of copies
without the system being affected
the genre definition remains
until the form of distribution
for the material implodes

to be in that
disappearing
which actively combats
the hanging of the individual
in places like
mazar-e sharif city square,
stammheim
nme

but still be an example
possible to study
and learn from

the situation is comical
and totally anarchic
just when the last beats
of the song have rung out

someone in the audience screams
sieg heil,
and manifests the
frustration and confusion that rules
at the core of a symbolic prank

7. unlistenable, entertaining
someone means that the drum beat, rhythm
is innate in mankind

a larger hall with sculptures
the sharp light
an early morning in may
seems to reveal the shame
of the originator
the sculptor, who is always someone else,
borrows details from the surroundings

the seventh recording
from moonlight club,
directly aimed at the organizers,
seems to ask
if the importance of performing
night after night
in the same configuration
the audio quality of the record
has deteriorated considerably
as if technology itself had revolted

certain really aggressive instruments
spite the machinery's performance
violating the agreement
to this night not generate distortion

8. also the white space,

the exhibition space
generates colored static

also that which has really happened
is combined with what
will never happen
and reduces emptiness
to a rhetorical tool
like zero in practice
more than anything else
is a very small number

for an artist the word hanging
has the significance
of (to hang paintings)
to install an exhibition
and put everything in place, to complete

to then,
immured in nervousness
await the moment when space
slowly becomcs populated
by people
until the point is reached
when one can say
everyone is here, we are complete

in the mass someone has to release the hand
of a beloved
a few unknown faces try
to reach each other for a long time
in the crush before the stage

9. *atrocity exhibition*
an infernal and final place

where symbolism and actual form
begin to merge

also classless
material has an origin
in its vulnerability

the testament's corner
the world corner
the edge of the book
written from within

the bibliography is impossible
all readers in the room
partake of the same information

the instrument is combined with delay

ceaseless delay
what does a guitar mean
the right proportions
of the sculpture
can no longer be judged

everything crashes inward
in the remnants, the masses
cannot be discerned
any originary form
not even physical decomposition

the idol argues for change
repeats himself to monotony
but also to comprehension, a track
to follow over and over again

the classification in the system
it is difficult to keep track of
if a biography is fiction
book, reference book

if here is such a space
this is not a "space"
knowledge of this place
does not accumulate
one cannot walk around
not remember more
it is not the point
that one should
force or break into
the room that reflects
one's body
one can stay

near the work
and observe,
leave when one leaves
and thereby also leave behind
almost everything

the subject (the subject)
is epistemology
and its exceptionally short lifespan
in the more than deadly shadow
of rhetoric

in this spot
in the radical work of sculpture
force takes place
not through a tough minted mass
but through an embodiment

that leaves invisible traces
in the physical form which
resembles the recognizable
the power to act is a privilege,
a profane mystery

"joy division convinced me
i could spit in the face of god"
neil norman, nme

ENEMY /
THE RED SHADOWS
IN THE VALLEY

.

approximately 30 miles away
two towers outside the sepulcher
a grey dove enters the flock
hundreds of white doves
get white feathers in forty days
every seventh one is a reincarnated soul
mazar-e sharif, the blue mosque
to read secondary sources

the fabric, the fabric
document and signs
through the landscape
slowly an experience
that has become shared

"in this country we drag
bloody goats after our horses"

in a body that is dissolved and reformed
is pronounced very early what
will later become known to all:
death is without syntax, choice

a poem about taliban
is without figure, choice

afghanistan and sweden go together
idle, concluded images
in the bookstores a particular color
mute and quick-drying
for immediate painting over of images
all the way back in storage spaces
hidden doors to secret rooms
where nothing remains stored

a movement that developed not only
backward but also away
turned away, not possible to regard
eye to eye

an attempt to rebound
make one's power vast and blind,
read in the opposite direction

"Decree, December 1996
2. Live and recorded music is prohibited
in stores, hotels, cars, and rickshaws.
We will make inspections within
five days 5. Kite-flying prohibited
6. Idolatry prohibited. In cars,
stores, hotels, homes and everywhere else
portraiture is prohibited."

the early central asian book
of crushed sea shells
discs with signs that dry
into the most fragile text
only shards can survive for thousands of years

early, at an impossible time
an important *serai*, or rest area,
for the camel caravans
along the old silk road

female professors who escaped kabul
established a university in bamiyan
most likely the most impoverished in the world

"in the north there is no public authority and in the south
there is only a very troublesome public authority"

viva academia,
kabul's new methodology
all the windows were painted black
no women were visible from the outside

indoors, without being allowed to see daylight
or mohammed's eyes

in the desert university knowledge was produced,
as was thought

in july the taliban went northward
from herat, cumulatively

the same day
two afghan un employees were found,
unhcr:s mohammed habibi and

wfp:s mohammed bahsaryar,
dead in jalalabad after
earlier having been kidnapped

in july the taliban went northward from herat

dostum fled to uzbekistan
and from there to turkey
dostum's flight demoralized
several uzbeki commandants

born in 1955 to a poor peasant family near sheberghan
ancestors who were part of djingis khan's hordes
the horses' exhalations in the morning cold

dostum was an appropriate leader
"in my innocence i asked the guards

if they had just slaughtered a goat"

mullah omar gave permission
to shoot people for two hours
even goats and donkeys
dogs ate of the carcasses and went mad

retribution,
for similar treatment
the taliban experienced in 1997
three shipping containers in the desert
since the prison in mazar was full
civilians, those dogged by misfortune
survival 1%

new names far down in the ground
and above ground – all names

the figure that is erected
when one person is selected from the group
taken aside and buried
after first having left behind
a dark pool puddle
orthodox as a halal lamb

either you become muslims
or else you leave afghanistan
if you flee upward we will pull you down by your feet,
if you flee downward we will pull you up by the hair

the saudi dissident osama bin laden's
training camp in eastern afghanistan
is struck by missiles

mullah omar's reply:

"if the attack on afghanistan
is clinton's own decision,
he made it in order to distract
the world's and the american people's
attention from the
shameful events in the white house
which have proven that clinton is
a liar and a man
without decency and honor"

"usa is the greatest terrorist in the world"

the international irritation

the most stringent resolution ever
threatened with unspecified sanctions

in a dramatic turn
wahdat's forces took back bamiyan
on april 21 1999

the taliban's complete isolation
pakistan's repudiation on october 12

the valley's red shadows


```
        (              )
     (                   )
   (                      )
   (                      )
   (      O        O      )
   (                      )
   (                      )
   (                      )
```

i want to protest against the destruction of
the gigantic buddhas in the bamiyan valley
for me it's like... i can't
understand why they have to blow them up
if we don't do anything and unesco and the un
aren't legitimate then what is
hans-eric wijmark, falun

hans-eric, hans-eric,
hans-eric, hans-eric,
hans-eric, hans-eric,
hans-eric, hans-eric,
hans-eric, hans-eric,
hans-eric, hans-eric,
hans-eric, hans-eric,
hans-eric, hans-eric,

"and each evening, the curtain covering
the face of the great buddha
is slowly drawn aside
on seeing the red-painted colossus
the pilgrims fall to the ground powerless,
one after the other"

there is in this poem a road to bamiyan
that is to say that valley in central afghanistan
where salsal and shahmama,
the world's two largest buddha statues,
erected sometime between the years 400
and 600 a.d., once stood

there is in this poem a road to bamiyan
which opens for the person
who hates literalism

or loves literalism deeply
the two gigantic buddhas
fired upon by the taliban
for almost three weeks
day and night, with anti-tank grenade launchers
are crushed to unrecognizable shards
again and again

the road to their destruction
and this poem's road
to both a gained and lost materiality

```
        (           )
      (               )
    (                   )
    (                   )
    (     O     O       )
    (                   )
    (                   )
    (                   )
```

in an
empire of signs
on a stretch of road towards
stone peace
state

the flag of representation
is incredibly red
incredibly red
and throws itself *throws itself*
in the wind

the sand is cold every morning
death comes with an ideology
the flag of representation is red
and subject to the wind

several signs make the book
that is a container,
a form for distribution

the word that takes the form of *word* is shouted out
sand blows into the valley and fills up
both wears upon and preserves the monuments
which have stood in a carved-out
niche in the mountain
for one thousand five hundred years

the smaller buddha
which the taliban, due to its size
may have considered a woman
the female word was accepted by the regime
but not the image nor the depiction

the way the buddha fell
the complete collapse from within
the execution,
was a direct consequence of
focused firing
on face and crotch

the taliban's extreme prohibitions against depiction
where no portraits, not even
a stylized human form could be permitted,
tempts poetry in modern time

the petitions against the bombing of
the bamiyan valley's wonderful sculptures
have like much other immortal fiction
ragged right margins

how does one engage the reader without prohibitions
to write poems is to illustrate
the book process, from cover to cover
a hermetic process
the borders are closed to the ravaged country
the regime in its blind goal to convince
must regard the population statistically
to write a collection of poetry is
to engage with the form
and to take form and give form to form a form of book
is to write poetry

the bamiyan valley's gigantic buddhas
the young, poorly educated militia
radical in its search
for meaning

it is not the case that the book
should be understood as autonomous
rather it is in itself a material
which in a simple, identifiable manner
presents its own place
as a form of distribution
and explains itself as a book
before the author ever can do it

through paratexts like isbn numbers,
logotypes, title pages,
front matter
alliances are formed
between the adjacent groupings

amir ul momineen
commander of the faithful

fundamentalist reading direction
sovereign in a particular character set

he who transforms monuments to signs
and fires upon his own interpretation

for a thousand years
the bodies functioned as monasteries

the story of the buddhas in bamiyan
is that the taliban in their literalness
did away with ornamentation on the sculptures
which since long ago
had housed buddhist monks
to emphasize the literalness
of their own practice, the metaphor's part in
the occlusion of a true message

and so on,

the story of the buddhas in bamiyan
is that sandstone crumbles,
entire mountains are worn down to desert
an explosion only hurries
the natural process
"the desert is our home"
our knowledge of it accumulates
thought must always begin again
from point zero, it does not accumulate
the stone's state is once again only
"a warning from the ice age"
the sculptor's philosophy
has always been subject to
the material

and so on,

the story of the buddhas in bamiyan
is that "the taliban's complete isolation
pakistan's repudiation on october 12"
truly created a desperate position
in a political and religious breakaway faction,
which claimed loyalty to a greater power
than north america and europe
the northern alliance's hold against tadzjikistan,
uzbekistan and turkmenistan
the difficulty in
controlling the opium plantations
that is to say get the farmers to cease
their deadly day job
god's presence in heroin addiction
why did the west not support this desire

to truly alter the conditions
for hundreds of thousands of drug farmers
why are stone figures so loaded
with the conservator nations'
monolithic anxiety

and

the story of the buddhas in bamiyan
is that their faces
which for hundreds of years have been gone
consisted either of mud and straw
painted in bright colors and decorated

or were carved out of wood,
and were therefore gigantic masks,
replaceable and seasonal

almost no researcher believes
that they were carved out of the rock
an earlier generation of revisionists
would in that case have carried out
a nearly superhuman and meticulous work
in their removal

and

during the occupation
a swedish delegation traveled to bamiyan
earmarked funds from the government and un
were to be utilized for an extensive renovation
of the two buddhas'
faceless faces

mullah omar states in an interview year 2004:

"I did not want to destroy
the Bamiyan Buddha.
In fact, some foreigners
came to me and said
they would like to conduct
repair work of the Bamiyan Buddha
that had been slightly damaged
due to rains.
This shocked me. I thought,
these callous people
have no regard for thousands
of living human beings
– the Afghans who are
dying of hunger,
but they are so concerned
about non-living objects
like the Buddha.

This was extremely deplorable.
That is why
I ordered its destruction.
Had they come for humanitarian work,
I would never have ordered
the Buddhas' destruction."

when the buddhist pilgrim xuangzang
year 630 a.d. visited the site
"with more than ten monasteries
and more than a thousand monks"
in addition to
an enormous reclining buddha statue
(which archaeologists today cannot find)
he saw the sitting buddhas in the valley
painted blood red and absolutely radiant
with reflected light

from the sunset in the desert
he saw the dead stone faces
so alive,
"decorated with gold and fine jewels"

the phantom image
of the outline of the process
could just as well be
the true profile

as much torn apart, bloody goat
as university educated female body
as much dostum
who was listed on seven different regimes' payrolls
and with his mercenaries
fought on the side of two religions

in the final stage of history
no one plays their actual part

extreme copy
indistinct original

the red morning
when the sun reaches the niche

nothing happens
but for the first time
the untreated mountain's interior darkness
is touched

the sculptural qualities
of the gravel, the pulverized amnesty
is judged based on context,

artistic valuations
never survive border movements intact

without kingdom
to look out from the vessel
that always is foreign, brimming
the thin metal, stone or skin
which besides taking the form of
the reality of rhetoric
supports the truly blind faith
that when something finally happens
it happens everywhere – simultaneously
and is no longer a violation

in an empire of signs
headed away from the command of representation
the artistic problem

which assumes the idea
of degree zero of responsibility,
a kind of pure position
or a chronic artistic filth
which must be made visible in order to be overlooked
documentary practice,
the stigmatized "social" material
is truly, historically speaking,
as omissive as it is investigative

poetry streams through the country,
through bamiyan
runs the river amu darya
the only way to not be captured in an image
is to constantly stay in motion
look at amu darya
it is not beautiful

but its stream leads out *out*
the landscape is lacerated
by parched irrigation streams
x's with pens, maneuvers
dashes and knowledge production
the words cut off sections
from other shores
the body disappears
and runs over to the other side

this is the amu darya poem:

```
(              )
 (      o      )
( 0            )
(    o   0     )
(              )
 (        0 o )
```

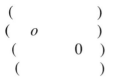

```
  (                  )
  (    o             )
   (          0   )
    (                )
```

(with the lost metaphors of violence
shimmering far down at its bottom)

the open space that remains
after the sculpture's removal
is like a person ready to receive anything
even though there is nothing left to confess
that was not already revealed long ago

the most common punishment is that a hand is cut off
to stone is to witness
the limitations of soft materials

in the oldest book information is locked
sea shells are crushed and form a mass
a designer's handling of the material
the process before text
is as important
as the text itself

by treating the turtle's shell
with a primitive chemical solvent

the book is here

it does not come from outside
it is a foreign body
that already exists
within

the form occupation takes
is the terrorist's language in the periphery,
the critical radical theory

the monuments' disintegration
in the symbolic core of a struggle

AWAKENED FROM *SLEEP*

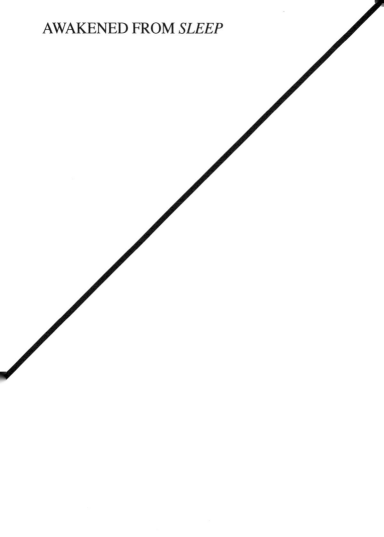

interview: john giorno

one can perhaps not speak
of anything as general as *sculpture*

john giorno, an *interview*

i am not quiet,
i have a conversation you cannot hear

i will edit your answers

the relationship between import and export
to order a book from amazon
in order to be able to *read him*

not refill, not fill up
not fill in or with
transition, editing
everything should hang together
more or less
the conversation should be intelligible

john giorno was the actor who slept
in andy warhol's *sleep*
he is an american poet
now living, new york

sleep is
a kind of
sleep into (come) crouched
over (bent) seated (sitting on) lie

(sleep) "sleep with me"
don't you think

assault (on the sleeping poet)

if this is a conversation
then something stands
in front of

you said you got something out of it
what exactly did you mean

the man lies down
in front of the camera

got what

it is the amer. poet:
poet voice

nothing more to say
i got nothing more to say

who says: that the artwork begins

the peace, the artwork starts *there*

in the constructive conversation
in the dialogue between
author and reader
artists and *the crowd*

106

ain't that sweet
impossible

andy war *hol* as in *holes*
andy war *hole*

said quiet *i*

i have a conversation you cannot hear

: war-ah-*hol* as in *holes*

giorno: i am a

this interview has started

the tape rolls

giorno:

when
when
he was first
he was first
when he was first
when he was first
shot
shot

i said to myself,
if these artists can do it,
why can't i do it for poetry

down
down
in the back
in the back
shot down in the back
shot down in the back
when he was first shot down
when he was first shot down

william burroughs, allen ginsberg,
brion gysin, john cage,
frank o'hara, john ashbery,
jim carroll, vito acconci, etc

william burroughs, allen ginsberg,
brion gysin, john cage,
frank o'hara, john ashbery,
jim carroll, vito acconci, etc

in the back
in the back

footnotes to the material

lyrics, sources, chants

who means that the text is not
an embodiment of
the literature

is crushed
toppled

placed in the window

john giorno was the actor who slept
in andy warhol's *sleep*
he's a poet pool poetry of
pool of blood

he wasn't dead
he wasn't dead
he wasn't dead
he wasn't dead
he wasn't dead
he wasn't dead

he just slept
seriously

in sleep

the dream of communication
the, *the communication*
which, yes

does not slow down the material, yes
which does not disturb the message
does not
disturb

i'm very happy
that you could make it
here tonight

which, yes
invisibly
is present, yes
yes which conveys
the message, yes

without disruptions

poetry loop poet
pool of

does not bleed at the moment of death
yes, which is clean, figurative
attached
lying

i said to myself
if these artists can do it,
why can't I do it for poetry

yes: it must really have been

the sleep
poet material
even in the deepest torpor
active as
potentiality
ricochet

why can't I do it
why can't I do it
for poetry

ha, ha

when he was shot
in the bed
i sängen
in the bed

it is also the sculpture that grows
in the frozen subject
the image is fixed and becomes
ghastly, ghostly
symbolic

the surviving myth
certain faces one cannot
stand to see
again
(again)
((again))

the things you did
in your everyday life…
you listened to rock 'n roll
from a phonograph.
the lp record
and sitting in
the living room
became the venue

the venue
a pool pöl of blood
clean in the eyes of the terrorist

111

as the hanging icon's gaze
transforms the human to
epic rigidity stone
ask what comes from within
no answer

perhaps literature is now
what is broken

can one say *broken apart*

can one say:
what the others call *form* i feel as *force*

through the nation
which does not only extend geographically
think of *the computers*

g: this is a golden age of poetry

everyday in '62 and '63,
andy and the others did
some fabulous work

the poem's relationship to
publication
is not investigated
in a satisfactory manner

what takes form
in the giving of form

this

        is

  poetry's   golden

a g e -   *era*

        they did what arose in their minds,
        and made it happen

        thing

        and in the image of nothing

        at the edge of
        the core
        the reader militia
        unusually quiet, conscious
        of what takes place

        write what counts

a general question: what is it that counts

        if this is an interview with john giorno
        material collected and edited
        cut from

        world of warcraft counts,
        for example,
        for many people

        it counts, it

second life,
the faceless dialogue
counts

i work in an airport,
it sucks *moans*
early mornings,
i'm still asleep when
i come to work

for many people life is better
on the other side

the world is getting empty of
e v e r y o n e i k n o w
o n e   b y   o n e
in every direction
t h e y a r e l e a v i n g
t h i s   w o r l d

in a conceptual world
but still not

will you be online tomorrow

14.30ish

suddenly it starts to rain in ashenvale
her char dissolves

stay up all night
and try to play *the game*

even dream about it

the swedish means
are useless
communication is limited
to this *realm*

the things you did in your everyday life
perhaps lay in the way of
poetic expression
the state of exception,
the swedish means
like a threshold in the symbolic shift
the empire of signs everywhere

the tools do not simply edit the object
but also point to it

and how did you develop this work
in order to explore other contexts
for presenting poetry

john's face
suddenly

and how

his face john's
suddenly shows

no

and how

his face
suddenly so calm

giorno: *the things you did*
in your everyday life

hung up an image

andy war hol
silverscreen

something so general
sculpture as representation
in human format

the passivity in
the viewing, the reading
on both sides of the border
a division takes place
of presence and absence

medusa's point in that
he who sees presence
is also present

john bursts into laughter
john's face looks so
calm

the event that has been promised

forces the viewer to remain

a fixed figure
threatened by dissolution
one cannot watch the film

john, have you seen the entire film

network, voice and death

have you

to be awakened,
the dream
"as if" it was a dream
makes itself impossible to convey through language
another reading,
even a completely different
grammatical energy
rules both in front of and behind
the horizon of understanding

your three absolutely favorite poets

john: but none of them are
any longer längre alive i livet

q: is this the golden age of poetry

a: this is the golden age of poetry

is it no longer a book that is called for

117

the form of a book
giorno's indifference
each realm's standardized
guardian language

it seems as if the information
flows freely

little codes for
action,
performativity

the warhol assassination

the text in an infinite space
is neither sign nor body
is not a part of outer space
the infinite creates its own meaning
through the symbolic entropy of writing

we all got terribly shaken

ask about the
strange knowledge
about poetry's totality of form
the interior

ask about *poets*
perhaps it is not possible to answer

is it

is
a body of a book clear evidence
that nothing has taken place,
except a change in ownership
and that nothing has been occupied
but still inseminated
with a completely new context

is that so

embodiment
through regime-, poet-, sculptural becoming
through (pe)trification
and hanging
appears like a basic condition
for the individual work of consumption
to appear meaningful

what would happen to him

temperature reveals the physical form
it is not a sleeping person
shown in the movie theater
but an illuminated film screen
ablaze with kelvin

would he stand up and walk again

would he leave us

to think of the book
is also to think of

the human body

cancer in my left ball
giorno's attempt to illustrate
his cell growth
the interior structure of the tumors
through methodical line endings
and repetitions in the text
the tumor is here also
a part of the literature

how close is it

how close
to create a new meaning among bodies
demands in part an awareness of
index, foundations of the principles of selection
as well as an actual selection

thank you so much
for your time and attention

containers in the desert
icon, idol
grit in the eyes
the morning after

poet pool loop of
book

stay,

that is how the book ends

thank you, my dear friend

it was totally my pleasure

to create a new meaning among bodies
goodbye
bye, bye
that is how the book ends

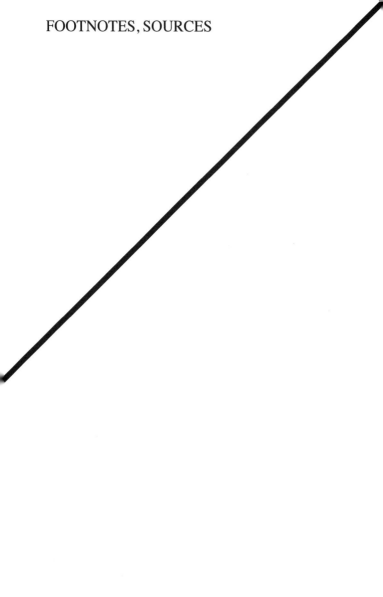

FOOTNOTES, SOURCES

1. The book begins

2. What Steve Sem-Sandberg on page 19 in *Theres* calls "Baader's conclusion" and was preceded by an intense plea from Andreas:

"Give me a context where I can act with the power of my complete self."

3.

4. A lecture
at the Museum of the Mediterranean in spring of 2006
Donny George, Museum Director at
the Iraq Museum discusses
how he and five co-workers
during the first twenty-four hours of
American occupation
had stayed in their museum
to defend its treasures
armed with sticks and shovels

The enormous building
had eight entrances
in addition to the loading docks
priceless objects
immured in the walls
they were not even behind doors
but lay hidden deep in the body of the building

When looters arrived a few nights later,
in numbers that altogether must have totaled
around three-hundred people,
everyone in the area
had been forced to evacuate
but American surveillance of the area
had not yet begun.

George divided, during the lecture,
the looters into three groups.
The first group stole
computers and telephones,
that is to say,
objects with an obvious value
to anyone.
The second group stole exhibition objects,
intent on the fact that it was a museum
they were emptying.

The third group
were professional looters,
aware that the objects on display
are not always the most valuable,
or rather, perhaps
are often copies of the actual objects
in this case hidden
within the museum itself.
These looters did not bother
with the exhibition spaces,
but simply blasted
(with the invasion's ongoing
explosions in the background)
through a wall on the north side
and decapitated stone lions on their way
down into the sealed vaults.

5. *Ornament and Crime* –
Description: Ariadne Pr, 1997. PAPERBACK.
Condition: Mint. Dust Jacket Condition: Mint.
Ornament and Crime contains thirty-six original
essays by the celebrated Viennese architect,
Adolf Loos (1870 – 1933). Bookseller Inventory #
BT0003011613

Adolf Loos, architect and author of *Ornament
and Crime* was a driving force during
the early 1900s. His ideas were extremely
significant to architects like Mies van der
Rohe and Le Corbusier. *Ornament and Crime*
became, along with Louis Henri Sullivan's "form
follows function" one of the slogans of the
modernist movement.

"Only a very small part of architecture belongs to art: the tomb and the monument." – Loos

"It is the pervading law of all things organic and inorganic, of all things physical and metaphysical, of all things human and all things super-human, of all true manifestations of the head, of the heart, of the soul, that the life is recognizable in its expression, that form follows function. This is the law."
– Sullivan

6. "THE STRUGGLE GOES ON"

"Andreas Baader was one of the two namesakes of the Baader-Meinhof Gang. A juvenile delinquent, Baader was drawn towards the leftist student movement because of the excitement, and the potential for violence. He was convicted of the 1968 arson bombing of a Frankfurt department store, along with his girlfriend Gudrun Ensslin. He escaped from police custody in May 1970 with the help of famous journalist Ulrike Meinhof, giving birth to the so-called *Baader-Meinhof Gang*."

The quote concerning Baader has been taken from "This is Baader-Meinhof" (*www.baader-meinhof. com*), a website run by Richard Huffman and which in addition to sections such as "RAF-timeline" and "Who's Who?" also features "baader-meinhof.com store" where one can order reproductions of wanted posters as well as stickers with the text "Ich gehöre nichtzur Baader-Meinhof Gruppe." These stickers were, according to Huffman, placed by the students of the day on their cars to avoid being stopped by an "overeager police."

> ### Ich gehöre nicht zur
> ### Baader-Meinhof Gruppe

7. The Swedish dramatist and his method were described in BLM 6/1982 in the following manner:

"We examine all of the body's expressions, biting, scratching, hitting, chewing, embracing, and CONTROL of all feelings, tics and tensions. We seek the means to show UNSPOKEN needs, partially as 'leaks,' where strong need erupts, 'sudden laughter,' 'sudden tears.' We construct certain movements and discuss which feelings the gestures, movements, inspire in the audience."

The actors then performed in

"... a 'real room,' with 'real things': bathroom, water, kitchen, sink, bicycles, brand name goods, specific paintings."

Even the audience was a part of this, they were in

"... an 'authentic' flat, no one could get closer, one could see in nearly everywhere, into the bathroom, the kitchen and out onto the balcony. It was practically a kind of superrealism. Floodlights illuminated an illusory view of a skyline."

8. "The Beach Book"

The laminated book body that
in direct sunlight
becomes absolutely burning hot
is mentioned in Gérard Genette's *Seuils*.

The English edition – *Paratexts*.

In another place in the book
appears an interesting quote by Balzac:

"Writers never make up anything,
an admission the great Walter Scott
humbly made in the preface where
he tore off the veil in which he
had long wrapped himself.

Even the details rarely belong to the writer,
for he is only a more or less successful transcriber.
The only thing that comes from him
is the combination of events, their literary
arrangement..."

La Fille aux yeux d'or

9. Publisher Bo Cavefors

To give voice to terrorists.

"Birgit Rohde, the Cultural Council's then-director,
indirectly managed to bankrupt one of Sweden's
most distinctive publishers when she rescinded the
promise that Cavefors could publish Strindberg's
collected work.

According to Eliasson the bankruptcy is caused by economic irregularities, but of 12 counts 11 are dismissed by the high court in Lund. The 12th count concerns Cavefors' transfer of approximately 7000 crowns to Germany without the approval of the Swedish Central Bank."

(*http://www.tidskrift.nu/artikel.php?Id=2495*)

10.

11. The "jerky" idol
is repeated into the image
by another (someone).

12. *Licht und Blindheit*
or *Sordide Sentimentale*
(SS 33002)
is a collector's rarity
printed in a limited edition
of 1578 copies

The seven-inch record is packaged
in a very unusual
brochure-like paper sleeve
that unfolds almost like a map.

In the material is a text
written by Jean-Pierre Turmel,
a painting done
by Jean- François Jamoul
and a black-and-white photograph
taken by Anton Corbijn.

In addition there are two small inserts –
an English translation of Turmel's text
and a blue, square piece of paper
with the text "Gesamtkunstwerk" and
"Avertissement."

The two known counterfeits of the record
are easily recognized if one knows
what the original looks like.

In the mid-80s
a bad bootleg was printed
on cheap paper and with a record label
that unlike the original
– white text on black background –
instead has an image of Medusa
in three different variations:
full color, blue or b/w.

The second counterfeit
has printed materials that qualitatively
are difficult to distinguish from the original.
The glue used for this copy
has not, however, yellowed and left stains
as the glue used in 1979
did in all known cases.

The counterfeit (2007) is also pressed
on red vinyl,
unlike the original's
classic black.

13. From Joy Division Central's forum:

OPERATION "LEST WE FORGET"

Jon: I'm a veteran of the ULU gig. My mate Paul
was at the Moonlight (first night) and Birmingham,
Julian Haynes was at the YMCA. The list goes on.
Let's compile a list of all the gigs and see if we can
match up a different person to each gig and then
people must write down EVERYTHING they
remember of that night. We need to do this NOW

as the 25th anniversary will be on us in no time at all and things will soon be lost in the mists of time. Here's to: OPERATION "LEST WE FORGET"

Erick the HalfBee: Incredibly loud, louder than anything I'd previously experienced, and most gigs I have been to since (I was only 14 at the time though). Ear-bleedingly loud guitar volume, and the drums pounded like gunshots amplified. It was too loud, if anything it might have been better quieter, would have given you a chance to hear what was being played.

Unknown: At 32 I'm still as enamoured and in love with the music as the 14 year old girl I was, hearing LWTUA for the first time. It has not subsided one bit, but increased with the availability of information

I have found over the years on the internet, music stores, and Ebay.

gravemaurice: My approach to music changed at a point from punk to something else, but I wasn't sure what it was. I was only 14. I bought all the JD releases such as the Earcom and Electric Circus stuff as well as the outright JD material. In later years when I had some cash and was working I bought the Factory Sampler 2 x 7", with the set of 5 stickers which no one ever seems to mention, but I then went on to sell them once I realised that they were not important to me – the personal memory of that gig means more than anything I could hold in my hand. This year aged 40 I went to the crem and looked for Ian's memorial stone. I found it and it was an extremely emotional point in my life. Not tearfull but more a feeling of satisfaction that I had somehow repaid a debt of some sort by making the effort to go and stand before it – full circle. I don't really know how to explain it – perhaps someone else may understand what it meant. Now I don't own any vinyl, I don't have any rarieties/ collectables – just those memories of how it felt to discover something so new, so strong, to stand before it and be part of it and to loose it so cruelly.

kered5: I actually taped a "gig" one night on my trusty Lloytron Cassette recorder strapped to my back, hidden behind my huge trench coat. As, I have posted before … the tape was long since lost and I can only assume that it suffered the fate of many of the gigs I recorded and got taped over by the Top 40 on sunday evenings. At the time … I can almost recall thinking … "Well that was a crap gig anyway, why would I bother keeping it?" However, I think I may have traded a copy with a guy from Beverley who I met at a record fair some months later … so it may still exist … there is hope.

brittgrrl: I just wish I could hit the rewind button. I am so jealous of those of you who were in the right place at the right time. I was born too late.

Duncan: Ian behaved a little differently during Atrocity Exhibition. Usually he would dance really wildly during the guitar/drums climax of this song. But this time he walked to the front of the stage and stared out at the audience completely still for about 15 seconds until a roadie came onstage and helped him offstage to hospital suffering dehydration and exhaustion.

Intermission: Well I never saw them as I am a mere 16 years old. But my father saw them twice. When he was stationed in Germany he saw the Koln gig and actually has some nice pictures and relatively good thoughts of it (and the beer, lol.) He also saw them in February of 1980 in Manchester (New Osbourne Club) when he was on leave visiting family members in Leeds. He too remembers the gig and also Ian's onstage antics. If only bands of such emotion and power remained … well Interpol is coming to Philadelphia Oct 14th …

Marko [admin]: Photos? You can't just mention photos like that – we need them for the site! Any chance? / Marko www.joydiv.com

14. News reporting,
the impossibility of developing
"a personal opinion."

Three people at random
who on one occasion or another
actually have protested:

Hans-Eric
Anna
Mattias Krohn

The protected original material
defended with a parenthesis:
(C) or (exceptions, exclusivity).

(A source of concern are those words and images

146

that must continue to be stored.)

WE MUST PREVENT
THE BLASTING OF
THE GIGANTIC BUDDHAS
IN BAMIYAN VALLEY!!!

WE MUST ACT NOW!!!

WE CANNOT WAIT ANY LONGER!!!

15. Narrative

Mullah Omar is one-eyed? ;)
and is purported to have said:

"Muslims should be proud of smashing idols. It has given praise to God that we have destroyed them."
(http:// www.gawaher.com)

Mullah Nasruddin is a well-known, comical figure in Afghanistan:

"A group of philosophers traveled far and wide to find, and, contemplated for many years, the end of the world but could not state a time for its coming. Finally they turned to Mullah Nasruddin and asked him:
– Do you know when the end of the world will be?
– Of course, said Mullah Nasruddin, when I die, that will be the end of the world.
– When you die? Are you sure?
– It will be for me at least, said Mullah Nasruddin."
(http:// www.afghan-network.net /Funny /1 .html)

16. Goat face,
(or no face at all)
rushes early in the morning
in circles in the dusty courtyard.
Not beaten, but baited
to harm itself
when it time and again
runs into the monuments
and the laughing mercenaries.

To further investigate:
Afghanistan Institute in Bubensdorf, Switzerland.
The institute can be considered
the "Afghan National Museum in Exile"
during the Taliban Period.
(http://cpprot.te.verweg.com/2005-January/000649
.html)

17. "a warning from the iceage"

Robert Smithson,
the American artist
who among other things made
Spiral Jetty and Amarillo Ramp
still saw, despite his enormous earthworks
the documentation of his work
as the central aspect of production.

So not the monumental
– stone, dirt, asphalt, gravel –
but what in a completely different place
– the gallery, the book, the journal –
attempted to recreate, or
rather, perhaps, mirror
what had happened in

a completely different site
in time and space.

The critic Lucy Lippard states
in the book *Robert Smithson: Sculpture* that:

"Had he not been first and foremost a sculptor
neither his work nor his ideas
would have been half so important."

The text and the idea
seem in this case to be
completely anchored
in something that
must assume a physical form
in order to be evaluated in its entirety

18. Dreams of earth and fire.

Nothing happens,
but for the first time the dark interior
of the untreated mountain
is touched.

Information
about the collapse of the skull,
the body which behind all pressure
long since ceased.

The reading is sheer terror:

Elevations: 53, 35, 2000
Numbers: 300000, 700000, between
three and four million
Years (in numbers): 1222, 827, 1998

19.

20. *Andy became overwrought.*
He couldn't believe it –
Marcel Duchamp!

I was there, and I got introduced too,
as a young poet.

21. Q : *What did you show in the Information show?*
(New York, 1970)

A: *Dial-a-Poem. Got a million of phone calls. And*
we had a room or alcove down in the main gallery
with monitoring telephones; and on the walls were
my silkscreen Poem Prints. Diane Di Prima wrote
a series of poems called Revolutionary Letters. One
was "How to Make a Molotov Cocktail". By chance,

*it was on the day The Weather People blew up the
IBM building. A newsperson happened to call Dial-
a-Poem and heard the Molotov Cocktail poem. The
news story headlines in the New York Times, Daily
News, and Post read: CALL THE ROCKERFELLER
MUSEUM AND LEARN HOW TO BLOW UP
THE IBM BUILDING next to a photograph of a
policeman shot dead, while talking on a telephone
in Philadelphia.*

22. J.M Exlibris 1881

23. Anyway, memories are distorted because the mind is like an imperfect crystal, or a curved mirror distorting the reflection. Emotions and paranoias distort the picture. As a Buddhist, I do meditation practice to purify the obscurations.

24. you can make
you can make
your body
your body
you can make your body
you can make your body
so light
so light
you can make your body so light
you can make your body so light

so light
so light
that it will float
that it will float
in air
in air
that it will float
that it will float
that it will float in air
that it will float in air
in air
in air

25. To create meaning among bodies
from always
insufficient information

everyday in '62 and '63,
Andy and the others did
some fabulous work

I was a kid in my early 20s, working as a stockbroker. I was living this life where I would see Andy every night, get drunk and go into work with a hangover every morning. The stock market opened at 10 and closed at three. By quarter to three I would be waiting at the door, dying to get home so I could have a nap before I met Andy. I slept all the time – when he called to ask what I was doing he would say, "Let me guess, sleeping?"

26. Says good-bye
bye, bye
after the tape recorder
has been turned off.